Why Do Black Men Like **Big** White Women?

Written by:
David (Goldie) Grey

So You Can Write Publications™
P.O. Box 80736
Milwaukee, WI 53208
Phone: (920)-821-3006

Library of Congress Cataloging-in-Publication Data

Love, David
Why Do Black Men Like Big White Women?
Published by So You Can Write Publications, LLC
06/15/2025

www.svcwp.com
home4writers@svcwp.com

ISBN: 979-8-9899762-7-0 (sc)

SO YOU CAN WRITE
PUBLICATIONS

Table contents

Introduction

Why Do Black Men Like Big White Women?

If you're like most men and women in society nowadays, your time is precious. I won't waste it here. I'd like to introduce this book by making a few key observances in dealing with mixed relationships and what specifically, men, "Black Men" are looking for in a particular type of relationship with "White Women;" and more specifically, "Big White Women."

Now, I know what you're thinking, you're probably thinking this is some bullshit that this writer is on. But let me tell you why this book is very important, because it will accomplish exposing almost every single thought of a Black man seeking a "full figured woman" of the opposite race. I will attempt to divulge Black men's intent and purposes in their pursuits of this particular type of relationship.

This is "jungle fever" x's 10. All jokes aside, just think of a time when you went out somewhere and you may have seen a mixed couple. Aside from the obvious, a "mixed couple," proportion wise it may not seem like the right fit. Here you have this big ole white girl, cute in the face and thick in the waist (as the brothers like to describe it as) in terms of compliment. But here she is being accompanied with this tiny little Black man by her side. Granted, some of us husky brothers will have a big white girl as well.

But my point is, and I know without a doubt that I am about to say what you are thinking whenever you have encountered and witnessed this in your life. "What is this dude doing with that big ole white girl?" There it is, I said it, what you were probably thinking anyway but didn't say it out loud.

This book will not only explore, poke fun at stereotypes, be provocative and asks questions that you're probably scared to say out loud, but in doing all those things this book will give you the practical suggestions and answers you've been looking for to address the practical problems every mixed relationship will face.

This book will thrill your heart because you will see the "big picture" of *'Why Do Black Men Like Big White Women,'* this book will uncover the truth.

A special thought, for the big and beautiful "full-figured" women of the world, long before a woman marries that desire surges to give herself completely to someone, to have a deep soul relationship with another, to be loved thoroughly and exclusively. The desire to pair off and settle down has been part of a woman's life for centuries no matter her size, race or age.

Some women are merely assertive without something to be assertive about. A female can talk softly if she has the power of self-respect. Eating or speaking, our attitudes are in charge. The woman most secure in a high position is usually one who would gladly be a subject. She commands best who can obey, she speaks surely who would gladly keep silent. "In quietness and in confidence shall be your strength..." Isaiah 30:15.

Chapter 1

I'm so lonely

Okay women, I'll be the first to admit it, men get lonely. Point blank! Sometimes we just get lonely; sad, because of having no friends or company. (Oxford University Press 4th Edition). Right now, I'm talking to all the women who just feel human out there. Try to understand Black man are humans with feelings, moods, and desires too. We do get lonely, lick our paws when all the bravado wears down, machoism wears off, we're only human.

Now, this is how it starts. Nowadays it's online dating apps: Tinder, Match.com, Plenty of fish, etc. You know what I mean, hookup sites. Long gone are the days of old fashion courting. Meeting a girl in the club, at the bar, check-out line inside the grocery store. We be like, "Hey baby, what's your name, you got a man? What's your sign? By the way, they call me Tyrone, but you can call me Ty for short." (Wink and a smile)

Now, you see the white girl... A brother bust his line, or via hook-up site. Either party is lonely, or why else would you leave the comfort of a nice relationship, date outside your race, or venture out and explore the wild side and catch "Jungle Fever?" FYI, Jungle Fever by definition means 'when a Black man dates a white woman, or vice versa' i.e. Tarzan meets Jane. That's the only way by example I know how to explain it.

Where were we, ok rather on-line or app you court the white girl, and then you think being lonely that's borderline desperate. I need some easy prey or rather easy lay, or even easy pay... referring to something that may possibly go past a one-night stand. Big girls hide your wallets!

Seriously, if I'm lonely like we all are at times, my standards go down a tad bit just to take in someone that I usually wouldn't embrace. I got an uncle that we call Uncle Lewis, he had a big white girl all my life. He used to say to me when I was a young, "boy, if she ain't white, she ain't getting in my pants tonight." His other catchy saying was and this one takes the cake (no pun intended), "she ain't a lady if she ain't 180." I actually like that one.

So, one day I conjured up the nerve and asked my uncle why Auntie Gene? Because I always wondered what did he see in that white girl, but then I'd notice, coming up, that my auntie was always taking good care of my uncle.

He said, "boy, that's the only woman who would put up with my crusty Black ass." Uncle Lewis continued, "I had fallen in love with that woman because she loved me first. It takes commitment to keep the good things in our life, and loyalty to hold them all."

*   *   *

Why do Black men like "Big White Women?" Would you be surprised if I said "personality?" But people really, can you honestly expect an answer to that in one answer? Come on now, of course not. That's the reason why I'm writing this book in the first place.

Hold on for a second, you must read this. Monique, for instance, she is cute as hell, cute ass face, full lips, cute smile, thick eyebrows, skin tone right, Indian complexion. Thinking if she lost 40 or 50 lbs. she'll be straight. Ideally, I estimated, she looked like 200 lbs., 5'7, cool as hell, but her body type... she was fat.

Some dudes just like fat women, they think big women are sexy. Some dudes might like that she caters to him.

You ever thought you wasn't good enough for someone, attractive enough to be liked or loved by somebody you deeply desired and wanted? Well, wanted them to like you, but to no avail were you even recognized by this person even if you had a million dollars hanging around your neck. Listen, we lower our standards in life a lot, and dumb down on the dating scene.

Desperate times always call for desperate measures when you're not feeling good about yourself. What you put out is what u receive. How am I going to love somebody when I don't even love myself? I sound like I'm trying to preach right now, the ghetto Dr. Phil, but seriously, you put up with people in life and their bullshit at times when dealing with a relationship because we feel a lack of value and self-worth about ourselves. Like this is all we can get. As the saying goes…. "I like whoever, or whatever likes me."

"I don't have a type."

My friend, let's call her Trina. How do I describe Trina, well, she's white of course for starters, middle age, meaning 30, and curvy (size 14), nonetheless, very attractive, but here's the kicker. Trina grew up in a home where she wasn't fed with compliments as a child in order to boost her morale and self-esteem about herself. It didn't help that she was a product of a single parent household being raised by her mother. A man's presence in her life growing up would have showed her how a lady is supposed to be treated but a man wasn't there.

Fast forward, Trina's grown now with 8 kids (all different dads) in tow… all by Black men.

11

Chapter 2

My Prerogative

"It's my prerogative... I can do what I wanna do, it's my prerogative... I can live the way I wanna live. It's my prerogative, I can see who I want to see...."

Who all know about that song? That was a R&B smash 90's hit by song artist Bobby Brown, but y'all get the point of what I'm trying to say, if not, then I strongly encourage you to continue reading along.

The reason I decided to call this chapter "My Prerogative" is basic, "Black Men want Big White Women!" Period. Don't run off just yet, I promise you I'm going somewhere with this hit song. Now, it's simple and I am going to break it down and tell you why, and these Black men whom are the minority in this pool, are those who say that "they" don't desire big white women are lying and subconsciously, it is just the opposite. Trust me I know!

Here's the breakdown. I'm going to give you readers a prime example: we all know who Kim Kardashian and the Kardashian broads, and if not, you must've been living under a rock for the past two decades. But anyway, Kim K, is the one who brought notoriety to herself and her family's last name was made famous by none other than her backside and the showcasing of its talents, but that's another story.

Second in line was her sister, Khloe Kardashian, thick Khloe the sexy siren being almost 2x the size of her sister Kim by virtue of her height, and weight. I'm not going to lie, Black men all over fell head over heels for these girls (what happened white America?)

Black men wanted and desired those women for none other reasons but their looks, which is the reason they became famous. And these two girls specifically are not the typical build or model type that are the customary girls you see on the catwalk. Those are the girls, ideally in the same arena, Black men want. I'm talking thick, big, curvy, shapely white women! We are drawn to big booties, big large butts, breasts, and the milk tone of white complexion.

I'm probably going to get jumped on for spilling the beans, I'm revealing a whole lot more about men psyche than Steve Harvey ever did in *'Think Like A Man, Act Like A Lady.'* I'm about to give y'all the keys to the security code in this book, but before I jump out the window... I'd like to ask, excuse me white girl but, "What's your name?" In Africa, a plus size woman is the status sign of great wealth, and the opposite is said to be true of a thin woman... the sign of poverty, a curse.

*　　　*　　　*

Ancestry

Let's talk about Big Momma, just for a second... here's a question? Did you know that, Black people ancestors are filled with very large Black women?

You'll discover damn near everybody Black either knows someone, or has someone in their own family tree some very large women they call "Big Momma" (affectionately) in our family. This is the same woman, or mother figure in such, is whom we all grew to love and cherish. Big Momma nurtured us, Big Momma loved us first, Big Momma was

13

always there for us, when the chips were down. Big Momma believed in us, she'll say, "Baby," while holding us so effervescently inside her arms, "it'll be ok." That everything no matter what we're going through is going to be fine.

I ain't going to lie, I miss that. Big Momma, where are you?! I'm going to tie all that into a big white woman, she gives us that same nurturing effect. That baby, everything is going to be fine type attitude. That same cuddling, like nothing we do can ever be wrong. We need that in our lives as men. Ladies, have you ever heard a man in your life comparing anything you do to his mother? I'm not saying all men are boys, but every man has a little boy in him.

So, our ancestors have these big women, we have big women in our family, we're used to big women, we're use to being around big women, period.

So, what draws us to big white women that's dealing with our ancestors? Forbiddingness, everybody wants things in life that they can't have, or should not have!

The fur trader wants the exotic animal. The poacher wants the Rhino horn. The Black man wants the white woman. He may not even love her per se, but he just wants her because he can't have her. But… the big white girl, on the other hand is willing to give herself away to the Black man.

Big girls do it better, but big white girls do it even better, and are easier. Hold on now sisters, I'm going somewhere with this. White girls just have to work that much harder. That's just the way I see it, now let me attempt to explain. I believe there's a statement on how they can keep a Black man satisfied. It's kind of like wrangling a bull, or catching a star in a jar. Big girls are easy and do it better.

There's a statement to be made here with you all. White girls, I'm about to be honest, Black men believe you feel you have to over compensate for us in order to keep us as your

14

man! Yeah, I said it… and now that it's out there let's break down the areas the Black man believes big white girls do it better at. Let's go there since it's on your mind, (yes, I'm a mind reader too.) Let's talk about sex, shall we. WARNING… tell the kids to leave the room, this is not going to be PG-13. White girls swallow. Y'all know what I'm talking about, needless to say, yeah, I'm going there. Can I be honest, can we have an adult conversation for a moment. Big White Women are more experimental, they are more open to accept another woman being invited into their bedroom. We like sex as men, we also like variety.

Chapter 3

Big Girls are Easy and Do It Better

For some reason it seems like all big white women are freaks, sex addicts. In the bedroom all inhibitions are let go of. Black men love it, just like that, it's time to test our skills out. Are you a flexible big girl, that's what we want to see? Will you say no, can I put it here, can I put it there, can I put it anywhere it will go? And big white girls are wetter than Black girls. I said it, I'm not trying to sound sexist, but this area in the bedroom is one of the main reasons Black men keep coming back to that "Forbidden Fruit."

Perhaps I should have named this chapter "Forbidden Fruit?" For some reason, Big White Women are more animated and vocal in bed in terms of stroking our ego. Black men could have the smallest dick in the world (contrary to popular belief), perhaps he missed endowment school, but that big white girl will still put forth an Oscar worthy performance in order to stroke that Black man's ego and make him feel like a man. This is very essential in sex period.

All men, the majority, would like to be appreciated and recognized for their contributions, and conquest inside the bedroom. Women, praise, praise, praise goes very far inside the bedroom, trust me I know. Ladies, I have a tip for you, as a matter of fact, several. If you want something done, or if you want something out of your man, ask while having sex. Catch him right at the point of climax, trust me, we will not turn you down, whatever you want.

Ladies, hear this, the same thing applies for finding out the truth. If you ever want to know something or find out something from your man, ask him during sex. You have to catch us right at that climax moment..... Girl, we will tell you "the whole and nothing but the truth..." But your questions must be straight to the point in order to get the "yes" or "no" answer. Big white girls spend their money with no restraint when it comes to taking good care of her Black man, HER BLACK MAN!

Yep, in her eyes we are made to feel like we are the big white girls prize possession. When u feel like that as a man it not only does something to your self-esteem and ego, but it invigorates your spirit as a man. I feel like a man when I'm with this girl. This is what I hear most Black men say when I poll over 100 Black men who were either dating or in a relationship with a beautiful plus size white woman. The consensus is in every way, big white girls go out of their way to do it better when it comes to pleasing their man.

Their mission is to take their Black man, some of whom has been stepped on and downtrodden by society, to regain his place and his position as a Black man in this white man's world. Assimilation may be key, which in turn often leads to miscegenation on the road to easy street down America's way. Black men want a big white girl that makes it easy and does it better on his journey in life. Destination to be determined.

*   *   *

The Forbidden Fruit

Genesis Ch. 3 v. 11 (in the Garden of Eden) and he (God) said, "Who told you that you were naked?"
Ch. 6 vs. 23-24 "Have you eaten from the tree, which I commanded you that you should not eat?"

17

One day, when I was much younger I overheard a conversation being shared between my mom and one of her friends.

My mom was the one giving her the advice... she told her, "girl, there are two key things you must do in order to keep a man from cheating on you. You must keep his stomach full and his nuts empty."

I was dying laughing, I ain't gonna lie. I almost got caught eavesdropping that day (of all times) because I was laughing so hard. Now the thing she said which resonated with me today was that, my momma, when she was done giving her friend a tad bit of advice on keeping a man, finalized it by saying, "girl a white woman gone steal yo man, he's gonna go after that "Forbidden Fruit" if you ain't handling your business in your relationship."

That brings me to this section, the "Forbidden Fruit." When I started this section, I quoted Genesis about Eve in the Garden of Eden, etc. Now the thing is ladies, some Black men may feel that white America doesn't want to see mixed couples, being a Black man with a white woman. Basically, it's a belief amongst older Black generations that white men are inferior to Black men. Perhaps that belief is still prevalent today?

Some of these stereotypes still exist in this day and age. There's phallus envy, athleticism envy, melanin envy, and so forth and so forth. With stereotypes embedded within the Black psyche on how white America feels about us, trust me every Black man knows of the negative stereotype that's been foretold by white America for ages. Ask yourself, what's born out of envy? Hate, mistrust, jealousy, and revenge.

Can it be, white women are looked upon in America subconsciously as "Trophies" "Armpieces" "Prizes" "Gifts," something very special? If some Black men relegate their

18

Black women as the Black Queen, then what do some white men relegate their white woman as? The White Queen? If some Black men feel downtrodden and stepped on by society and in our psyche their lives the stories of your years of slavery. In such, could we be trying to exact revenge subconsciously by going after and stealing the white man's prize, his white woman! I use the terms loosely because I believe Big White Women exact revenge subconsciously upon disseverment of their own race for not being socially desirable because of their size, and thus give themselves a way to the opposite race as a form of get back.

In closing this chapter, I would like to pose this question. Could the white woman be the Black man's status symbol in this day and age saying, and I quote "White man I have made it, now I'm able to sit at the same table as you, and partake in your cake and eat it too!" (Figuratively and Literally)

Chapter 4

The Breakdown

Black women vs. White women, and the untold truth. (The Breakdown. This is how I feel, God forgive me, I'm going in... I'm going in... I'm going in.)

Latina women, my mother once told me "red bones (light skin girls) was the shit back in the day until the Spanish girls came around" (Redbone will have your mind gone).

America had raised its population to lust after white women. The media taught us that being white was the epitome of beauty. Black people grew to adore that long, straight hair, light colored eyes, slim bodies, and tanned light skin.

The problem used to be back in the "daze" that the white girls just weren't built like Black women. Most didn't have the thick bodies, wide hips, lips, and phat ass most Black men desired. And maybe we love Latina's because they are "the best of both worlds." They have the long straight hair, light colored eyes and permanent complexion of a white woman well-tanned. They are also thick, with the lips, wide hips, and phat ass most Black men love!

We used to feel like Black was the thing to be... "the Blacker the berry, the sweeter the juice" pun intended. "I want a sister. I can't dismiss her; Red beans and rice didn't miss her." Come on now, you remember that Sir Mix a Lot song *'Baby Got Back'* which was in essence paying homage to all the beautiful, endowed, Black women out there that America dubbed as plus size. But hold on, stop the press white America.

White Woman has mounted a comeback, they have rallied back as the prize.

"If it ain't white it ain't right."

"If it's snowing, I ain't going."

The snow bunnies (white women) have taken "their place back on the mound." The media has sensationalized and praised the booty, and white women who were once frowned upon for being full figured and plus sized have torn the world upside down. White women: Ashley Graham, Kim Kardashian, Coco, Iggy Azalea, and the list goes on. Now, get this, in Africa, the motherland, a plus size woman is the status symbol and sign for Great Wealth, Prosperity and Blessings. The opposite is said true of a thin woman, the sign of poverty, and a curse.

It is decoded in our genes, that a part of us wants a big girl, (A woman that's endowed with plus size). After all, nobody wants a white girl, if nothing else just to say that he had her for conquest purposes of his own.

Do the math, big girl (endowed with big breasts and big booty, and pretty face) + white girl = right girl in Black man's eyes!

*　　*　　*

Snoop's outlook on why they love us.

Fat white women = low self-esteem, no self-worth, not feeling accepted or successful enough for white race, dating out of pity, Black men are her preference, she knows we got that Mandingo and know how to work it. We are ruff necks, go hard, we are affiliated with power, being strong, and demand respect. We like white women... Good credit!

21

They're submissive (don't like confrontation but they'll get argumentative after years of being with you after they think they figured you out or know who you are.) Or, molded you to who they wanted you to be, nurturing. Adventurous, they love thugs, they like the mystique of the Black man. Curiosity... They like being dominated. Gullibility, you can't fuck a sister in the ass, but white woman you can. Good background, strong family ties, inheritance (business passed down) etc. Career driven.

White women do stuff outside the norm of our race. For example, Black women don't like getting their hair wet... Going swimming is out of the question. Black women don't like the outdoors, going camping, fishing, or nature hikes, shit like that. Most Black women live up to these stereotypes. Therefore, the aforementioned Black men are longing for these types of experiences in our lives. It reminds me of our boyhood. Whereas, some of not most, white women grew up as a child experiencing those types of things, going fishing, camping, hiking etc.

Unlike their counterparts. Sisters don't normally have those adventures growing up. Namely, because young Black girls grew up getting their hair perm and relaxed. As children they were told not to get their hair wet. So that is why a lot of Black women don't know how to swim. Yeah, I said that too and it's the absolute truth. Tell the truth, shame the devil. Meanwhile, we went back on course talking about why these Black men yearn and crave that Big Ol' Beautiful Milk of Magnesia Sista.' And no pun intended to all those who may be Lactose intolerant.

Chapter 5

Internal Dysfunction

Inside the physic of Black men therein lies the need to be accepted by the establishment or the societal standards of America. The questions of Black men are; white men can I sit at your table? This age-old dilemma still exists and thus, Black men see their key to being accepted is by having a white woman. There's also rebellious nature. Emmett Till, was killed because he was accused of whistling at a white woman. Black men have within their minds the notion; not the white man's bitch!

When white America looks down upon their full-figured plus size women and discards them, Black men have the notion; one man's trash is another man's treasure... we want her because you (white America) don't! Black men who feel the NEED to have a woman of a different race, I believe that they have an identity problem; like a dog wanting to be a cat, like a fish wanting to be a bird and like a bear wanting to be a rabbit. Some Black men want to be a white man as I stated before so eloquently.

And they feel their only avenue to achieving this is to have a white girl as their significant other in order to fit in. The easiest route is one (a white girl) who will accept you. That commonly occurs with one low self-esteem, or expectations to have a man, of any race or background who will genuinely treat you right and keep you in first place. Now, seeing that I already gave you my version of what Internal Dysfunction means... Internal Dysfunctional by the way of medical dictionary definition means; Mental health (psychiatric or psychological) disorders involve disturbances in thinking, emotion, or behavior.

Small disturbances in these aspects of life are common, but when such disturbances interfere with life, they are considered mental illness or mental health disorders. The effects of mental illness may be long-lasting or temporary. These disorders are caused by complex interactions between physical, psychologic, social, CULTURAL, and hereditary influence. I personally wrestled with this oddity and rather complex and taboo topic.

In often trying to understand Black men and why we chose to date and seek a significant other outside of our own race? And more specifically why do Black men target/ gravitate and pursue a special or distinctive type of white woman? Albeit, structurally build women of their race. Just some skinny, tinny, itty-bitty, white girl/woman won't do it! I'm telling you, Black men for whatever reason are in fact infatuated, attracted to entrances, by Big and Beautiful white women.

I'm talking cornbread fed, farmers daughter type, "Thick in the waist and cute in the face." Black men just find bigger white women irresistible for whatever reason. Within this book I've tried to dismantle and unmask ideological reasons and issues regarding Black Mojo, a magic spell, hex, or charm (magical power). White women, particularly big white women, have Black men. Black men feel they might need a big white girl because she's a lot less stressful. People, my dear readers, I have left you with the ball in your court to try and draw your own conclusion as to why do Black men like big white women.

*   *   *

24

Trina

Let's face it, and keep it real; can I keep it real? Let's talk about this girl named Trina. For example, if I will.

[Disclaimer: all Characters mention in this book and their likeness, thereof are completely fictional. My intentions and purposes are to dissect this truth, stigma, and stereotype in the Black Community of "Why do Black Men Like Big White Women."]

Trina is an example that I'm using of a typical middle age plus size white woman. Trina is very self-conscious and insecure because of her weight. The voice of white America Cosmopolitan, Vogue magazines along with various blogs and tabloids say you're fat by portraying in the media a false image and identity. The Barbie doll syndrome, why hasn't America made plus size dolls for kids?

Instead of fashioning children's ideals of what an average woman looks like. Trina hides her weight and tries to disguise her appearance by wearing dark clothes not flattering to her weight. Like a moth attracted to a flame the Black man is conscientious of white America's disdain for her outcasts and sees Trina, as someone who can somewhat relate or find commonality with. A rebellion of love, a forbidden dance of sorts. This is all subconscious, stating a rebellious reasoning to miscegenate.

Black men are attracted to big white women with low self-esteem. A predatory instinct that is also primal within the self-consciousness of a Black man. Strong women are intimidating to most Black men, if not all men, men will never admit this. The Black male, with a lesser degree in class or status in white America, who averages somewhere around 30,000 dollars a year at best per employment. Let's go with a guy named Andre, by example. Andre chooses my homegirl Trina and they hook-up via friends. My homegirl Trina, plays the back role or the wingman position on date night where Trina is somewhat forced to entertain somebody else.

Trina and Andre, both are second fiddle if I must go along the lines of the echelon of beauty and class in this country. Andre, has no abs, Trina, has no beach body, the perfect match. Insecurity shrouded in love. "Why do Black Men like Big White Women?" Because they're juicy. Black men have a disposition that a Black woman will not take him or accept his condition if he is down and out, doing bad, down on his luck.

That is a belief, some may view as a stereotype. But overall, if one feels that they are outcasted or not worthy enough for a certain type. You'll look elsewhere for love. Another race, another type, another experience. As human beings, there are 4 things we require in life:

- Shelter -
- Food -
- Security -
- Love -

Like ants, one ant ventures off scouting for greener pastures and when he returns, he tells the other side, (the wild side). I'm talking about "Jungle Fever" y'all. So, we, Black men venture off for that prey and specific type, The Big White Woman in search of her sweetness in order to have our needs met. But most importantly, to find security. You don't feel insecurity in life in a relationship where someone desires you as much, if not more than their equal.

We have an image of strong Black men… and oddly enough, King Kong was viewed as a villain, but that white woman felt secure in his hands, mystified, terrified, enchanted, aroused, hypnotized and attracted at the same damn time! For the plus size average woman who has been ousted by society and made to feel because of her size she is not worthy, she has a Black man somewhere desiring her because of that sense of insecurity! And it works both ways, Black men feeling like he fell short of Black women standards will veer off elsewhere to be easily loved and accepted for who he is, for who they ARE. Two loves, two lives, two worlds, two races, opposite welded together in insecurity, rebellion, and hope.

Chapter 6

The Cons & Pros Part 1&2
Part 1: Cons

The pros and the cons to loving a Black man. The status quo, first off, you're going to be judged based on an "interracial relationship." Let's just clear that up and address that issue. The elephant in the room is some people are just plain racist, biased, ignorant whatever. I know it's 2025, and times have changed, and to see an "interracial relationship" pretty much everywhere and still be ignorant to this new day and age of social acceptance.

People need to just downright get over it! The reality is, sadly, that everyone's not ready to accept your relationship. And you can be judged based on someone's preconceived ideology stemming from racism.

Secondly, a Black man may feel out of place in dating outside of his race and exhibit symptoms of a relationship withdrawal. Real Talk! I am not making this up because I can't make this up. Black men, not all Black men, experience and exhibit signs of withdrawal. It's a push back as if a Black man has the weight on his shoulders as if he has betrayed his own race by choosing to date a white woman. A Black man may feel he has to down play exhibits of affection when he's with his significant other when amongst his counterparts' race.

In order not to offend his race. So, you can be cutting short or getting cut short on deserved affection due in part to your man's subconscious fear of not wanting to offend his race. Believe me every Black man is aware of history surrounding the past of how Black people, Black men

28

particularly were treated for dating outside of their race. So, there can be restraint on the level of love you should be receiving, but due in part to an inherent fear of castration or disappointment. Black men could be substantially withholding back on loving a white woman the 100% that she deserves in a relationship. And he could fear vice versa that he deserves.

The cons of this situation could also be mistaken in a non-cultural connection. Whereas white women and Black men don't always culturally connect and that's important in any relationship, is your connection outside of the bedroom. Culture is defined as per Webster's Dictionary definition: "particular people or group with ideas, customs, skills, arts, etc. of a people that are transferred, communicated, passed along, as in or to succeeding generations."

Black women are super women due to their historical plight in overcoming the monstrosities of racism. PLUS, women suffrages all of which Black women overcame and still overcome. However, Black men are tired. They deal with the "angry Black woman syndrome." Only way out of pain is to share pain! Broken, taking off the mask and sharing pain leaves the Black man vulnerable... white women will deal with this resentment from a Black man's pain. And his anger can be expressed by passive aggressive behavior.

This passive aggressive behavior will be him cheating and possibly verbal abuse. "Resentment," is what some Black men carry and that's because they may feel deep inside that they're betrayed their own race, by being in a relationship with a white woman. They pick petty arguments in an attempt to lash out. The topics of the argument can range from your weight which wasn't an issue when y'all laid down and he met you. It could be your dress, style, food quality, any of these minuscule reasons.

The reality is, aside from being sorry as a man, we lash out, it's not you it's us! Black Men have issues that historically haven't been addressed and that poison seeps into our relationship.

Part 2: The Pros

Here I go again nonetheless, this is where this book gets really interesting, nail biting, and a bit intriguing complex at best!

Let's talk about the word cultured just briefly for a second, I'm going somewhere with this. Cultured means "refinement, or experience outside of your norm" more less, a change in the narrative of life. By dating a Black man, you are an essence exhibiting that you are cultured. A woman whose objective, open-minded and of substance wherein you're not conforming to the typical stereotypes of yester years, wherein it was viewed as taboo and not socially accepted to mix one's race.

Long gone those days - this is a new era-social consciousness that is well alive and kicking. Black men have style, substance, swag, soul and transformative powers to adapt. Most Black men are inherently physically strong. On a micro level to be given, Africa, you have a land with all its resources. I do realize that the comparison is a stretch. A leader to a degree if in fact this is what you desire. Every Black man has a tribal instinct to be a leader whether that's head of the household and relationship.

This is a middle finger to the masses and all the haters. One man's trash is another man's treasure. When white America frowned on "plus size women" white women in particular, Black America accepted the wrongfulness of this stereotype and viewed "plus size white women" as beautiful. I'm talking Black men, who loved those beautiful white sisters' whom their counterparts' white males viewed as fat, overweight, grotesque etc.

"One of the greatest inventions of the twentieth century, is the African-American male invented because Black masculinity represents an amalgam of fears and projections in the American psyche which rarely conveys or contains the trope of truth about the Black males' existence." The Pros, sexual assumptions that fetishize Black male bodies as aggressive, hypermasculine, and overly sexual are undoubtedly true!

In layman's terms, putting this simply, white women, a Black man will rock your world inside the bedroom! He will have you calling out his name, "Tyrone, Antwan, Jamal" whichever guy you chose, you get the point. So, it's about the penis, but then it's not. It's more about a sort of softness of a Black male character that he exhibits towards you when he is expressing genuine true love.

Chapter 7

Part 1- Self-Confidence and Self-Esteem

Self-confidence has attraction value by its own virtues. It is a signal of resources. Black men, scoring high on self-confidence who may earn significantly more money than Black men with low self-confidence are less likely to approach or go out with a plus size woman especially a plus size white woman.

It is a signal of self-perceived mate value. Another study, for example, discovered that only Black men high in self-confidence approach physically attractive white women more for dates, regardless of their own level of attractiveness. Black men who suffer Low self-esteem, in contrast, avoid approaching attractive white women because they think they will strike out in pursuit of that Barbie Doll type.

Self-esteem is a psychological term that refers to a person's sense of his or her value or worth. Self-esteem is typically measured by asking people about whether they are satisfied with themselves; whether they feel they have a number of good quality traits and are able to do things as well as other people and whether they are proud of themselves, feel successful, and have respect for themselves. Self-esteem has been related to personality features such as shyness, behavioral outcomes such as how well someone can perform a task under pressure, thought processes such as the likelihood of taking blame for failures, and health behaviors.

Among Black men, for example, research reveals that those who experience a bit of impotence, or erectile dysfunction suffer a tremendous blow to their self-esteem.

There's an adaptive reason for this link: Failure to perform sexually historically, would have jeopardized a Black man's reproductive success. Conversely, few things raise a Black man's Self-esteem more than a fresh sexual conquest of an attractive woman.

That's why Black men drift to other races for women in order to be accepted, to regain a sense of dominance and control as a man. Objectively, some Black men view a full figure white woman i.e. a big white girl as easy, yup, they sure as hell do! Big white girls are often viewed and construed as easy! Among Black men, evolution has forged adaptive links between esteem and sexual success.

Sometimes these links, as we will see, can go awry in the modern world. Although some standards of a female beauty are culturally variable such as the preference for relative slenderness or plumpness many are universal. Ladies, features with Black men that have universal sex appeal include clear, smooth skin, plump lips, clear, large eyes, good muscle tone, sprightly gait, symmetrical features, and a low waist-to-hip ratio all of which are associated with fertility.

Studies of how women feel about their bodies reveal their overall sexual attractiveness, as well as their specific body attributes such as waist, thighs, and hips. Men think because a woman's appearance provides such a bounty of cues to her fertility. Black men have evolved mate preferences that, perhaps unfortunately, give tremendous importance to a woman's physical appearance. It is a psychological fact of life that women are sometimes treated as sex objects just as men are sometimes treated as status objects.

On the positive side, having a good Black man can provide a plus size white woman with a rush of confidence. Capturing the Black Panther, or, more of the less settling and having an "at least I have a man" attitude. My auntie Gene, who happens to be a beautiful full figure/plus size woman said to me: "in times of feeling less confident, overweight, unattractive, etc. it has been nice to know that someone else found me attractive and still wanted me." Although it is true that a woman's body image is affected by her weight and body shape.

Researchers have found that it is also greatly influenced by her own personal perceptions about her body and what it should look like. Concerns about body image exist in women of all ages. In a nationwide survey of thirty thousand individuals ranging in age from fifteen to seventy-four, 55% of women expressed dissatisfaction with their bodies. Among adolescent girls, body image is adversely affected by exposure to beauty magazines. Among women in their late fifties and older, body image tends to be linked more to their health than to how their bodies compare with the latest winner of America's Next Top Model.

There are also cultural differences in how satisfied or dissatisfied women tend to be with their bodies, with media saturated Western countries expressing more dissatisfaction. Even within the United States, studies find cultural differences: Black women in particular are much more satisfied with their bodies than women of other races and ethnicities. Not surprisingly, body image concerns play a major role in propelling women to buy and try all the latest diet advice and supplements, a $50 Billion-dollar industry, in North America alone.

A poor body image causes some women to develop eating disorders, including anorexia nervosa (self-starvation) and bulimia nervosa (binge eating and purging). I'm going to tell you straight up that no Black man wants a bone but a dog. We like our women "thick" cornbread fed, "red beans and rice didn't miss her" (a quote from Sir Mix-A-Lot song; *Baby Got*

Back') y'all remember that song. And less well known is the fact that how a woman feels about her body significantly impacts all aspects of her sexuality.

Studies among some U.S college women reveal that those who rate themselves as unattractive are less likely to have a sexual partner, probably because women who are dissatisfied with their bodies are self-conscious and experience anxiety about someone viewing them naked. Consequently, they sometimes avoid rather than pursue sexual opportunities. Even amongst college students who are in sexual relationships.

People think full figured white women with negative body images have less frequent sex and are more likely to experiment sexually than their positive-body-image peers. That's what Black men, at least believe. Of course, there are always exceptions. It's a common belief amongst Black males that some, if not most big white women with poor body images deliberately seek out sexual activity and relationships with Black men to try to make themselves feel better about their looks.

And in addition to altering how willing a full figure white woman is to engage in a relationship and experiment with the opposite sex, a negative body image can adversely affect a woman's actual sexual response too. I've already explained how some people, contrary to most Black men believe that full-figure white women with poor body images have lower sex drives, more problems becoming aroused, and greater difficulty achieving orgasms.

An associate of mine conducted a study where she had 85 college women come into the lab one at a time and privately fill out questionnaires about their sexual functioning/ relationships and their body images. The body image questionnaire asked how they felt about their weight and

35

Part 2

A body image is paramount and plays a major role in why Black males particularly like big white women. The way a woman views herself, how she feels about her own sense of self-worth, her appearance, her weight, her size and height, hair, the color of her eyes, her skin tone. It is too pale, too white. The more so many white women perceived herself to be less attractive than she was ten years earlier, the more she reported a decrease in sexual functioning among so many other ethnicities of women over the past ten years.

The reverse was so true. The whiter women judge themselves to be attractive, the more likely she was to report an increase in sexual response and sexual activity over the previous ten years. It should be noted as factual per scientific studies that suggest. When a woman is too focused on how her body looks during sex, be it as it may, short, tall, skinny, and small, Black or white. And how her partner may be evaluating her body, she becomes distracted from pleasurable sensations that can help her become aroused and have an orgasm.

TRAINING women to refocus their attention on pleasurable sensations during sex is a key part of many successful sex therapy techniques. Challenging the woman's often unfounded beliefs about what her body should look like and helping her to view her body in a more accurate and objective manner are also effective treatment techniques. A study of 32 clinically obese middle-age white women who underwent a 31-week weight loss program demonstrated the link between body image and sexual functioning.

In addition to losing a substantial amount of weight, women completing the study experienced huge improvements in body image and sex drive, and actually engaged in sex more frequently. When they were later asked why they thought their sexual functioning improved after the program, almost 3 quarters of the women said that it was because they'd felt better about their bodies. Way too much has been written about the media's role in contributing to full-figure white women's dissatisfaction with their bodies. As a society, we seem to be on a first name basis with women who are celebrated primarily for being thin and pretty, but does anyone know the name of any most recent woman to win a Pulitzer Prize for literature?

Me, my point exactly. Of course not. Again, let's revisit a closer look at the images against which women usually judge their bodies. Runway models are typically five feet ten or taller and average 120 to 124 lbs. in weight. Many young (and not so young) women dream about looking like them. But the reality is that only 5% of all women have the genetic make-up to achieve that body type-no matter how much they diet, exercise, undergo plastic surgery, or develop a health-destroying eating disorder.

Pictures of waiflike movie stars, with shoulder blades poking through their sweaters, grace the gossip and fashion weeklies, looking as one feminist website calls it, "impossibly beautiful." So impossibly beautiful, in fact, that photo altering software programs are used to slim and tuck cheeks, arms, stomachs, and legs while magically expanding bra cup sizes. The ideal has become so pervasive in the entertainment industry that in some cases, photos have to be altered to make women's hips and collar bones less pronounced.

Even Barbie can be implicated. As it turns out, researchers have actually calculated that if Barbie was life size she would weigh no more than 110 lbs., which means she would have so little body fat that she probably would not even be able to menstruate. The moral of this chapter (s) that I chose specifically to write, is all about full figure white women building a healthy sense of self-esteem which often comes from taking stock of your personal strengths and abilities, being content with who you are and what you have to offer the world.

But instead of focusing inward on oneself as a person, some people focus outward on external comparison to create their sense of self-worth. And seek someone who will validate them (a Black man) some desperate, some not. Instead, love yourself more, and most importantly know your worth. Cheers, go head white girl, you can do it!

Chapter 8

Defense vs. Deception
Defending Against Deception

Although some Black men sometimes succeed in deceiving some full-figured white women who perceived herself undesirable. On the contrary, it would be flat out wrong to conclude that a majority of plus size Caucasian women i.e. full-figured white women as a whole are all passive dupes in Black men mating games. These women know that some Black men have a powerful desire for casual no strings attached sex type relationships.

In fact, some developed sophisticated means of identifying deceivers. Research shows that women are superior to men at reading nonverbal signals such as facial expressions and body movements. They decode facial expressions, evaluate vocal tones to assess sincerity, and gather information about a man's social reputation and sexual history. Some spend hours discussing specific conversations with their close friends who help to evaluate a man's intentions.

Another key tactic that some women use involves insisting on a longer courtship before consenting to give up "the cookie" as Steve Harvey would say. All in all, that men typically desire, in one study we asked women and men about the likelihood that they would have sex with someone who happens to be of the opposite race and ideal weight that we're attracted to. If they had known the person for varying lengths of time ranging from one hour to five years. Whereas most Black men were likely to have sex after just one week, most big white women preferred a less wait. Giving the cookie up the same day or week.

Imposing a time delay before having sex allows a woman greater window of assessment and evaluation, a strategy in part designed to weed out deceivers. Most plus size white women also have specialized emotional defenses that protect them from being deceived. Research shows that these women become extremely angry and upset when they discover that these men have deceived them about the depth of their feelings, in order to have sex or gain sorts of material, transportation, shelter money.

These emotions cause these women to etch those deceptive episodes in memory, attend more closely in the future to possible instances of deception. And possibly looking at all Black men as deceivers of the coveted full figure white woman. Evolutionary psychologist Martie Haselton discovered yet another defense women have to avoid being emotionally deceived by Black men; the commitment skepticism bias, consider a concrete example: On a second date, a Black man declares to full figured white woman that he is deeply in love with her.

Based on this cue, what is the correct inference about the man's true state of commitment to the woman? There are two possible errors of inference a woman can make. One error would be to infer that he is telling the truth about his love, when in fact he is practicing the art of deception. Evolutionary logic suggests that being deceived would have been the costliest error to women over history. Women deceived in these ways would have risked an unwanted or untimely pregnancy; being inseminated by a man with inferior genes; and possibly raising a child without the help of an investing father.

41

So, evolution has fashioned a particular psychology in women, according to this theory: a commitment. The commitment skepticism bias serves an important function. It helps women not to be overly impressed with easy-to-fake signals, such as verbal declarations of depth of feeling. It requires men who are truly committed to display additional commitment cues over a greater length of time. And it causes Black men who are truly interested in just a "quickie" as the youngsters say, to soon tire of the delay and move on to more gullible, exploitable, or sexually accessible targets.

At this point in time, plus-size white women and Black men are the end products of the perpetual arms race of deception strategies and deception detection defenses. Some plus-size beautiful (full-figure) white women succeed and deflect their deceivers; and some fall victim to Black men's very deceptive charms. What would you do?

Despite the frequency of deception, most lies turned out to be modest embellishments. Men exaggerated their true height by only half an inch on average. Women underestimated their weight by roughly 8.5 pounds. Most online daters appear to deceive in ways that are "close enough to steal" rather than grossly mischaracterize themselves on qualities that would soon be discovered in a face-to-face date. There are always exceptions though.

One man said he was three inches taller and eleven years younger than he actually turned out to be. One woman said that she was thirty-five pounds lighter than her measured weight turned out to be. On the whole, though, the mischaracterization told by most online daters were slight exaggerations rather than bold faced lies. Deception in dating is an equal opportunity tactic-both men and women do it. On qualities that are easily observable, such as height, weight, and attractiveness, people sometimes lie just a little.

Outright lies, such as a short man claiming to be six feet tall or a heavyset woman claiming to be 125 pounds, will be easily detected, and the deception will backfire as soon as the two people meet. However, some deceptions are difficult to identify. Qualities such as income or social status are generally tougher to verify, which is why at least some internet dating sites now contain other information. Some even check to see whether the person has a criminal history, a fact that some people may inadvertently omit from their dating profiles. Most women seek some kind of sexual connection or emotional involvement with a man before consenting to a relationship.

From an evolutionary perspective, this is emotional wisdom that women have inherited from their successful maternal ancestors. A man's emotional involvement is conditional, particularly his genuine love provides a powerful signal that he will stick with her through thick and thin, through health and sickness.

Time provides the best chance that he will devote his commitment, provisions, and protection to one woman and her children. Most Black men not in love feel freer to flirt from woman to woman. Black men are sometimes baffled by women's desire for emotional involvement and love. You think saying "I love you" to a woman to thrill and entice her isn't necessary anymore. But that's not so. These three words I-Love-You as a Black man, we still do believe that those three words still have a tonic like effect on white women especially those being heavy set in stature.

In fact, studies reveal that emotional deception by Black men is an astonishingly common tactic for persuading big white women to have sex with them or get money and other favors. In one study, I asked 240 women and 239 men to describe ways in which they had been deceived by members of the opposite race in particular. I found that full figure white women reported having been deceived by Black men in the following ways:

*Concealed a serious involvement with another woman (9%);
*Lied about how attracted he was to the other women (26%);
*Concealed emotional feelings for another white woman (25%);
*Exaggerated his work ambitions (21%)
*Exaggerated how kind and understanding he was (42%);
*Misled her about how strong his feelings were for her (36%);
*Concealed the fact that he was flirting with other women (40%);
*Misled her about the depth of his feelings for her in order to get sex (29%);
Misled her about the level of his long-term commitment to her (28%);

These percentages are likely to be underestimates of the actual rates of deception. In another study of 112 Black men, 71% admitted that they had sometimes exaggerated the depth of their feelings for big white women in order to finesse her.

various aspects of their sexual attractiveness. Then, in rooms by themselves, the women read an erotic story about interracial couples and rated how turned on the story made them.

Women who felt good about their bodies experienced much more sexual desire and inner feelings in response to the stories than women who felt bad about either their weight or level of attractiveness. The women with poorer body images also reported having lower desire in real life situations with their partners. Noted, these were women of all races and body types. If a woman's view of her body changes over time, it can also change her level of sexual desire and her body's response during sex. Dr. Patricia Barthalow Koch and her colleagues at Pennsylvania State University assessed changes in the sexuality of more than three hundred middle-aged women across time.

They found that over a period of 10 years, approximately 57% of women reported a lessening of sexual desire, 58% reported actually engaging in sex less often, 40% reported enjoying sex less, and 32% reported enjoying sex less, and 32% reported having difficulty with orgasms. The researchers then look to see what might explain the decreases in sexual functioning among so many women.

Chapter 9

Final Thoughts

Noted psychologist Dr. Sigmund Frued, once stated "hedonism is in theory exhibitionist and are those who have suppressed their sexual appetite and hidden desires for so long. And when the right person shows up in your life they bring it out of you!"

A real man isn't scared of strong, smart, and independent women. I will tell you, psychoanalysis Dr. Freud, I believe, was wrong in some of his undertakings and sexual analysis. I'd dare to say as a researcher and expert on this book, Black men do have penis envy, for good penises that respect women and are not threatened by people who are smarter or more powerful than them. And I believe based on my undertakings and research that is what a good man is.

Let's be honest about something too when it comes to why Black men like big white women. It's an economic question and issue too! First off, it depends on where you live in this country.

Secondly, how you're doing financially. Now we're cooking with oil, people. I am exposing this topic, and I believe I've hit the spot! Also, I believe the more Black men are threatened, the worse they become at masculinity. I exposed a lot of truths in this book. Struck a lot of nerves, got on a few people nerves with the statements I've made (fact findings). But, all in all. I believe humor is how you get people to step outside their comfort zone. To change their minds or at least pause to look at things, topics, and people in a different way.

Humor is the way that people escape. Humor is how you can embrace the enemy of the unknown. *'Why Do Black Men Like Big White Women?'* Instead of approaching that statement and putting it off on the big white women insecurities issue. How about why do Black Men Like Big White Women, has something to do with Black mens own insecurity issues and lack of confidence? Black men supposed to be this, supposed to be that, you can fill in the blanks with whatever stereotypes. But in the end, like all humans a Black man just wants to be happy, loved not forgotten.

Like any and all human beings. But it is complex in part dealing with miscegenation. Inhibitions are let go when you've already crossed over into interracial dating i.e. relationship. Breaking all traditions, rules, expectations and norms. Kudos to those that have. Not conforming to society standards of yester years when interracial dating was so taboo especially if one's partner does not conform to the adherence of beauty. Beauty is in the eye of the beholder. In fact, biracial dating of plus size women is the norm in this generation in this day in age.

Dating a Black man puts you into a place where it isn't familiar ground. Am I right? Who you are is the question. Some Black men do want to earnestly know what's inside your head. Might I recommend reading books together and discussing them. One has to be an asset instead of liability in any endeavor of a relationship. Albeit plus size, white, Black, whatever. Honestly, I found some Black men do actually think that nobody wants a big white woman.

However, on the contrary most women do want somebody who they can believe in. Black men believe in the beauty of the body or the self-confidence of a woman secure in herself.

Chapter 10

Conclusion/Epilogue

'Why Do Black Men Like Big White Women,' specifically amongst all other races and types of women? Is surely one of the most fascinating, complex, and enigmatic questions facing the psychology of human motivation. Throughout this book, I have explored many motives from the frantic desperation to regain some measure of dignity after being spurned to the soaring heights of the consummation of true love; from the altruistic motive of boosting a partner's self-esteem to the selfish motive of exacting revenge; from the thrill of adventure to the dark side of deception; from the mundane motive.

Although for economy and clarity of communication, I have parsed the reason why Black men have discrete motivations. It's important to acknowledge that what drives a Black man to want a big white woman is often more complex and multifaceted, containing varying combinations of motivations. A Black man might want to gain status among his peer group posing as "playa-playa." A Black man might have this attraction, a prospective partner appearance ignites his desire and because he's unhappy with his current relationship to a Black woman.

We must recognize too that Black men's motivations sometimes conflict with one another. Trust me, I have tried to examine the magnificent diversity of Black men's motivations through several theoretical lenses. One is placing Black men's sexuality within an evolutionary perspective framing it in the context of the bewildering variety of adaptive problems ancestral Black men have repeatedly confronted over eons of deep time. Once upon a time ago in Africa-big (plus size) women were a sign of prosperity. This is a Black man's cultural belief subconsciously and consciously. I hope that the unique confluence of these multiple lenses has revealed many more facets of Black men's motivations than would any single conceptual lens.

I also hope that beyond these theoretical lenses, multiplicity of motivations has sprung to life through the experiences directly and eloquently described by men and women who graciously agreed to participate in my study. A full-figured white woman recounting sex with her partner albeit a Black man as "the fullest flower of the blossom of our love" may capture more of the true experience than the abstract triangular theory of love.

This gives credence to the saying we all know and love "once you go Black you don't go back." And to all the plus size, full-figure, curvy Caucasian women out there who suffered feelings of humiliation and degradation after being emotionally and sexually deceived by a Black man brings the phenomenon of these exploitations to life more than my theoretical analysis of why deception is so prevalent in human species. It should be noted that not all Black men conform to this stereotype or my opinions and research herein this brilliant masterpiece.

Lastly, I want to share with my readers this quote from the song artist Lizzo, she was asked this question during an interview she was giving if she had advice for any woman struggling to achieve full body confidence; "self-love and self-confidence is a personal journey. You are never going to believe it until you believe in yourself. But luckily, now we have so many people you can see yourself in. You can go on the internet or look on TV and see people who were really marginalized and underrepresented in the past. That's the most important thing. You have to see yourself, find yourself somewhere out there. You've got to go on that journey and I believe in you." So, does this author.

Epilogue

Recently, I'd engaged in a conversation with a friend about a woman he was dating that was a plus size white woman, middle age with a biracial child. My friend is a Black man, middle aged and slightly big built. The woman in this relationship was grief stricken with guilt mixed with insecurity because of her weight. They'd been in a relationship for over two years now. He told me based on my inquiries into their status that this woman whose name is Wendy has developed an anxiety and fear that one day her boyfriend Leon would leave her based on her weight.

He said she wasn't comfortable going out in public. He'd mention one particular incident that struck me as alarming and painful. They went out to the Cheesecake Factory restaurant wherein he had free dinner passes and he wanted to use them before they expired. He almost literally had to pull his then fiancée out of the car when they arrived because she had become so overwhelmed with fear she refused to go inside the restaurant to eat. When they finally got to the door she'd made an abrupt stop right in the doorway, turned and did an about face and sprinted back to the car. While leaving Leon alone standing there at the front of the restaurant doorway in amazement at how fast she can actually move.

"She blew right past me," he said before continuing, "and then when I followed after Wendy and reached the car I asked why did she leave? Wendy responded in between her tears and catching her breath with, "stop yelling at me. I'm scared and afraid that everybody in the restaurant will be looking at me.?"

Reader's, I can't make this up. This is all true and very much personal, these life experiences and testimonials about why do Black Men Like Big White Women. Hold on, in case you're wondering what Black men think, in terms of desiring a big white woman! Trust me, readers get your antennas up. This is the part where you're definitely going to want to pay attention to.

Basically, what Black men think about in regards to having a relationship with big white women. Straight to the point! She's EASY! Yeah, I said it! And I'm going to say it again so you reading this can hear me loud and clear. Obviously, I don't care who I offend! But most Black men think big white women are just plain easy! I'm talking about a relationship. And when I say EASY, I mean some Black men think just because you're BIG- you must be vulnerable, unsecure, impressionable, naive, x'10. And insecure.

Note; to big white women, everywhere (all over the world), please show that you have confidence. Show confidence. Sweetheart, YOU ARE BEAUTIFUL and guys think this but, even if you don't have the confidence, fake it till you make it- just don't be some one's presumptuous target! Ok, they also can sense you as a prey and easy lay if you do portray these characteristics of vulnerability, insecurity and naivety. I'm just saying, I discovered through investigating numerous Black men in dealing with the big white women the conclusion.

Black men do think that big white girls are EASY and stupid! I'm just warning you, heed this message. These guys who criticized me and tried to critique my writing told me not to put this book out. In an attempt that "I am giving up and divulging too much game and street knowledge" in other words referring to "Game." If you've ever been on a journey to an uncharted territory in your life and needed directions to reach your destination. You would undoubtedly use GPS in order to find your way. This book, and these chapters are just that. This book is what you need. These chapters are in fact a tour guide into the psyche of Black men. Those of which are involved in interracial relationships with plus size white women.

Dare I say this quote from a song; "everybody needs somebody to love!" The honest to God truth is, some Black men do sincerely love big white women! The fact of the matter is, whilst some Black men think big white women are easy, realistically, the opposite may be true. To expound, basically most Black men desire food, music, sports and sex in whatever arrangement, those are the basic essentials in life. When it comes to dealing with men in any and all races you keep his nuts empty and his stomach full as a rule of thumb when you're dealing with any Black man in any relationship.

Now, as an author I share with you this tidbit of advice, I was raised in a household full of Black women, things I heard over time are being exposed and shared with you through these pages. In particular, Black men who think big white women are easy when I say the opposite is true, I mean the Black man who desires this certain demographic of women is easier, these types of Black men who seek an "easy" woman are the type of men who have low goals if any in their lives.

Note to all women; RUN FROM THESE TYPE! These "so-called" men, boys in men's bodies, are those who seek out big white women who can take care of them, baby them, enable them, shelter them, and feed them. Well, damn, you might as well go out and buy yourself a dog. At least they're cheaper! Those Black men, who target certain women based on body types, race, and vulnerabilities, are the same Black men who are fragile, vulnerable and scared of a REAL

WOMAN who will stand up for herself and be independently strong. Self-motivated and courageous!

Go head girl, with yo big ol' fine self. Bring out the inner boss in you. My hopes in writing this book is to inform, motivate, inspire and provoke intellectual adult conversation on this subject.

Acknowledgements

Most importantly God, for always showing me a way and not to give up. My loving kids, it is you all who I inspire to be better for. And to So You Can Write Publications.

SO YOU CAN WRITE
PUBLICATIONS®

www.sycwp.com

"Where the writers go…"

www.ingramcontent.com/pod-product-compliance
Lightning Source LLC
Chambersburg PA
CBHW032035090426
42741CB00006B/827